Sufism

The Sufi Path to Spiritual Awareness

Table of Contents

Introduction 1

Chapter 1: What Is Sufism? 5

The History of Sufism 7

The Spirituality behind Sufism 13

Sufism vs. Islamic Sects.................................... 14

Five Pillars of Islam 14

Chapter 2: Sufi Beliefs and Practices 17

Components of Sufism.. 17

Pillars of Sufism 19

Teachings of Sufism.. 21

Practices of Sufism 23

Chapter 3: Sufi Psychology.................................29

The Facets of Sufi Psychology 31

Jihad in Sufism 35

The Levels of Nafs.. 37

Chapter 4: The Wing of Love............................41

Love in Sufism 41

The Concepts of Ishq and Mahabba
in Sufism 44

Chapter 5: The Sufi Path..............................51

The Four Spiritual Paths of Sufism.................... 53

Conclusion...63

References..66

Introduction

Sufism is more than just a faith or religious belief. Adopting its teachings can change your life and make you reach a higher level of consciousness. When you truly understand Sufism and embrace it, it can transform your life around.

The book begins by introducing the concept of Sufism and explaining in detail what it means. We will then take a trip back in time to discover its origin and history. You will also learn about all the thinkers who contributed to spreading the teaching of Sufism all over the world. The book also covers the spiritual beliefs associated with Sufism and the most influential figures in its history. Although Sufism is always associated with Islam, it is still different from the religious sects. The chapter ends by shedding light on the differences between the two.

Sufism stands out with its unique beliefs and practices. The book will first introduce the components, teachings, and pillars of Sufism, then explain in detail different practices and the common places where the followers perform their ceremonies.

Many people regard Sufism as a spiritual practice, but it is also linked to psychology. The book will cast light upon this connection and explain how one can reach self-realization.

Sufism has its understanding of love. You will discover how the followers perceive love and introduce the different concepts associated with it. Some of the most famous poets were Sufi practitioners, and their poems were inspired by their beliefs. We will include some of the most poetic romantic verses and explain the significance of love in achieving spiritual awakening.

The last part of the book will present the goal of Sufism. We will explain the different paths of Sufism and why every Sufi should follow them. You will also learn about the practices associated with the paths that will eventually help you achieve spiritual awakening.

The book contains all the information a beginner needs to understand the concept of Sufism. We used simple language to avoid confusing or overwhelming the reader and to present it in an interesting way to make it delightful to read.

Begin your Sufism journey and prepare yourself to be forever transformed.

Chapter 1

What Is Sufism?

Sufism, also called "Tasawwuf," meaning mysticism, is an ascetic and mystic tradition in Islam. The word Sufism is derived from the Arabic word "Suf," which means wool because back in the day, ascetics wore wool attires. Sufism focuses on introspection to develop a connection with God which is a similarity that it shares with Hindu practices.

Although not all Muslims believe in Sufism, it is still very popular and practiced by millions worldwide. However, it is more common among Muslim Sunnis. Sunni is one of the two sects of Islam practiced by the majority of Muslims, unlike its less traditional counterpart, Shia. In the Western world, there is a misconception that Sufism is a separate practice from Islam, but it has always been associated with it, and some even consider it a part of the religion.

Islam is a monotheistic religion that believes in one God, Allah. Sufis (the people who practice

Sufism) believe that this practice brings them closer to Allah. They establish this connection with the Divine by Muraqaba (meditation), Dhikr (remembering God), or by seeking the help of their "murshid," the spiritual guide in Sufism.

Sufis believe that Sufism is integrated into Islam. They consider Sharia (the religious laws of Islam) the body and Sufism, the soul. Sharia is the foundation of Islam; one can't practice religion without understanding the rules that govern it. On the other hand, Sufism is the spiritual side of the faith which brings peace and joy to one's life. Practicing Sufism through meditation and Dhikr raises one's consciousness to have a better understanding of the Divine and develop a close bond with Him.

Unlike other religious traditions, Sufism is very diverse and flexible. It doesn't include rigid beliefs or practices, for instance, obligatory praying five times a day. However, practices in Sufism aren't governed by strict rules and can change depending on the culture and traditions of a country.

The one thing that all Sufis share in common is the concept of Shiite Sufi or "tariqa," which is the order in Sufism. Each Sufi region has its own orders, and the Mevlevi Order is the most common one among Western practitioners. Followers of this order perform "Hadhra," which is a ritual that involves dancing and music.

In Sufism, the master or teacher is called Shaykh, Arabic for an elder person, and the student is called mureed, meaning "the one who seeks."

Sufism exists to please Allah and lead Muslims back to their fitra, which is their most pure and innocent form. One must let go of their ego and love for the material world and surrender to God.

The History of Sufism

Historians and Sufis can't agree on the real origin of Sufism. Some say that it originated a few centuries after the death of Prophet Mohamed (peace be upon him), between the eighth and tenth centuries. It only became a common practice in the 12th century when it was developed into orders. Many Sufis agree with this timeline since it confirms that Sufism belongs to the school of Islam. However, there are others who believe that Sufism predates Islam and originated during early Christianity in the Middle East in Egypt and Syria. It is believed that this is where Muslim Sufis based their beliefs.

The origin of Sufism can be debatable, but its connection with Islam, for many Muslim Sufis, is unquestionable. Ibn Khaldun, an Arab and Muslim thinker and philosopher, believed that the Sahaba (companions and followers of Prophet Mohamed, peace be upon him, who supported him at the beginning of Islam) practiced the beliefs of Sufism before the term was coined. Later, as more people began focusing on the material, the term Sufism came to describe the spirituality of Islam.

In the tenth century, many writers were publishing manuals that sum up the laws and practices of Sufism. The most influential manuals are Risâla, an Arabic word that means "the message" by Arab and Muslim scholar Al-Qushayri, and Kashf al-Mahjûb, which means "Revelation of the veiled" by Ali Hujwiri who was a Persian Muslim mystic whose work had a huge impact on Sufism. Persian poet and Sufism practitioner Jami, Abd-Allah ibn Muhammad ibn Al-Hanafiyyah was the first person to be referred to as a Sufi and is considered the father of Sufism. Abd-Allah was the narrator of Hadith (recorded words of Prophet Mohamed, peace be upon him), so he was very respected in the Muslim community.

Abu Hamid Al-Ghazali was a Persian and Muslim polymath and a Sufi practitioner. In his books "Alchemy of Happiness" and "Revival of Religious Sciences," he stated that Sufism was based on the teachings of the Quran, and many of its beliefs are directly derived from the Muslim holy book. Therefore, Sufism doesn't contradict Islam, and one can even argue that Sufism, in some way, completes Islam. Even though some people try to challenge this belief and say that Sufism doesn't follow Islam, scholars use Al-Ghazali's work to refute their ideas. Al-Ghazali's books have recently been translated into English to give more people the chance to truly understand Sufism and its relationship with Islam.

In Al-Andalus (the Muslim regions in Spain), Islam was the predominant religion in the ninth and tenth centuries. Muslims weren't very welcoming of Sufism as they believed these philosophical thoughts contradicted their religious beliefs. However, in the twelfth and thirteenth centuries, thanks to Al-Ghazali's work, people changed how they viewed Sufism and began embracing it.

Ibn Masarra was a Muslim philosopher who lived in Al-Andalus and was one of the first Sufi practitioners in the region. He began the first school of Sufism and helped spread the belief all over Spain. Many scholars agree that Ibn Masarra had a huge impact on Sufism in Spain, and it reached its peak popularity in his lifetime. However, after his death, things took a turn, with his work being destroyed and his followers persecuted.

In the twelfth and thirteenth centuries, Spain saw a powerful philosophical movement with more people showing interest in Plato's and Aristotle's work, along with Muslim philosophers like Ibn Rushd, Ibn Bajjah, and Ibn Tufail who incorporated the religious views of Sufism into philosophy. During this time, Sufism was widely practiced in Spain and other regions in the Middle East.

Abu l-'Abbas ibn al-'Arif was one of the most famous Sufi figures in Al-Andalus and the founder of the tariqa. He was influenced by Al-Ghazali's books and introduced them to Spain and other Western regions. One of his students, Ibn Qasi, built a Sufi monastery with other Sufis in Silves, Portugal.

Another prominent Sufi figure in Spain was Ibn Arabi, whose work focused on the mystic and metaphysical. He was interested in the human spirit and how one can attain perfection. After his death came Ibn Abbad al-Rundi, who was a famous Sufi figure as well. Unlike some who came before him, his work was more accepted in the Muslim world.

One can't talk about Sufism without mentioning its most popular figure in history, Persian poet Jalal-al-Din Muhammad Rumi. Even those who aren't familiar with Sufism have heard about Rumi and his poems. Rumi was a Sufi practitioner until his death, and many of his poems were inspired by Sufism. He was also the founder of the Mevlevi order.

Although there are many prominent and influential figures in Sufism, there isn't a person or a group that one can consider founders. However, Al-Hasan al-Basri is credited for setting the foundation of Sufism and is highly revered among Sufis.

He was one of the first people to practice "zuhd," or asceticism, and his work contributed to the development of Sufism.

Sufism found its way to India as well. There were many influential tariqas that were established in India, like Qadiriyya, Suhrawardiyya, Naqshbandiyya, and Chishti, which was the predominant order.

Nowadays, the most common Sufi orders are:

- Suhrawardiyya
- Shadhiliyya
- Qadiriyya
- Oveyssi
- Ba 'Alawiyya
- Nimatullahi
- Naqshbandi
- Khalwati
- Chishti

Sufism has spread in many regions around the world, especially in Africa, where the belief has accommodated many of their mystical traditions.

The Spirituality behind Sufism

Sufism is a peaceful practice that is about love and gratitude. It follows Prophet Mohamed's (peace be upon him) teachings that include loving all God's creatures because they are a reflection of the Creator. Sufis don't harm others even if they wrong them; rather, they turn the other cheek. They don't focus on other people's flaws and mistakes. Instead, they look at them with love because they see God's light running through them. When you see God in everyone you meet, it makes it easy to forgive them and overlook their flaws. Sufis are meant to be one with God through love and suffering.

Sufism is more than just a belief; it is a way of life where one lives in harmony with God's creation. Sufis believe they should live with virtue and must constantly purify and cleanse themselves from the sins and evil in the world.

Being one with the Divine is a concept that exists in many beliefs and cultures. It is the idea of looking into one's self and finding something deeper and more profound than you, the Divine.

For this reason, you don't have to be a Muslim to practice Sufism as it is more diverse and universal than one religious belief. Islam is a religion, but Sufism isn't. Although this argument might separate Sufism from Islam, which many religious scholars refuse to accept. They look back at the history of Sufism through the work of Al-Ghazali to prove that it came from the Quran.

Sufism vs. Islamic Sects

Sufism isn't a sect of Islam. Many Sufis regard it as practicing Islam with chanting and meditation. This is different from Islam sects Sunni and Shia, which don't include singing or dancing and only focus on the five pillars of Islam. Islamic sects don't practice or believe in mysticism or being one with the Divine.

Five Pillars of Islam

1. El shahada (a declaration of faith that Allah is the only God and prophet Mohamed, peace be upon him, is His prophet)
2. Salah (praying five times a day)

3. Zakat (giving a portion of your money to the poor)

4. Sawm (fasting in the month of Ramadan)

5. Hajj (holy pilgrimage)

While Muslim Sufis practice the five pillars of Islam, Sunnis, and Shias don't practice Muraqaba or Dhikr. Muslims find spirituality in fasting, praying, and other Islamic pillars. They also believe that they will encounter God in the afterlife, unlike Sufis, who believe they can reach God in this life.

There are many people who don't follow Islam but practice the teachings of Sufism, like love, openness, forgiveness, and becoming one with the Divine.

Some people regard Sufism as a part of Islam, while others see it as a spiritual concept based on Islam but as its own separate religious practice. The argument about its origin and connection with the religion will not go away. Although the majority of scholars associate it with Islam, the concept of Sufism can stand on its own as the spiritual belief that connects and unites us with the divine.

Sufism has managed to change and adapt to different cultures. The flexibility of Sufism and its connection with Islam are why this belief is popular among Muslims and non-Muslims alike.

Chapter 2

Sufi Beliefs and Practices

Although Muslim Sufis practice the five pillars of Islam, they have their own traditions and teachings that set them apart from the religion. All their practices enable them to establish a connection with the Divine. Even their spiritual beliefs that focus on loving and accepting all God's creatures are meant to get them closer to Allah This chapter will focus on the components, pillars, teachings, and practices of Sufism.

Components of Sufism

Sufism is practiced through tariqas or orders in many Muslim countries. Strict rules don't govern these orders since they are developed and adapted according to the culture and traditions of the country. Each Sufi order has its own structure, but its main component remains the same. There is the Murshid who acts as a spiritual guide to his follower who is called Murid. Before the Murshid begins guiding and teaching, the Murid must first pledge bayah (allegiance) to him to establish a relationship between him and his teacher. The Murshid guides the Murid to connect with and become one with the Divine. No one can join an order before pledging bayah to the Murshid.

Unlike priests, Murshids and Murids have more freedom and are allowed to get married and have children. Sufism doesn't require them to give up their lives and lead a monastic life. Your life won't revolve around the order, and you won't need to make drastic sacrifices; it's merely an aspect of your life.

There is a chain of succession in Sufism where one starts as a Murid and then moves up the chain of command. A Murid can one day become a Murshid and have their own disciples. After the Murid learns everything about Sufism, they are ready to pass their knowledge on to the new followers. However, they must gain their Murshid's permission first. In the hierarchy, the Wali or grandmaster is above the Murshid.

Sufism based the relationship between the Murshid and Murid on Prophet Mohamed (peace be upon him) and his sahaba (companions) when he initiated them and went on a spiritual path together. Just like the Sahaba learned everything about Allah and Islam from the prophet Mohamed (peace be upon him), Sufi followers can learn everything about their beliefs from their teachers. The sahaba also pledged bayah to the Prophet to join him.

Pillars of Sufism

Sufism based its pillars on the teachings of the Quran. The Quran instructs Muslims to be humble, do charity, and be truthful.

Humility

Humility in Sufism is more than just being humble. When a humble person embraces humility, they don't become egoless. They abandon one ego and embrace another. They may not show off or brag in the typical sense, but they are aware of their humility and feel it makes them special. For instance, a person praises themselves for being polite to the waiter and thinking, "I am a very humble person. I don't think anyone else treats people like I do." Or when you compare yourself to others and believe your humility makes you a better person. This means that the ego is still inside of you. A person who brags about their big house or expensive car is no different from a person who brags about giving money to charity. Both have surrendered to their egos.

True humility is being aware of the ego and that it can take various subtle forms. Once you accept you are no better than anyone else and that your ego can deceive you, it fades away, and you can become truly humble. Sufis believe that humility is necessary to reach the Divine.

Charity

Giving money to those who are less fortunate than you and feeling good about it isn't charity. Helping someone and making them feel indebted to you isn't charitable, either. In Sufism, charity is giving away something to another person and feeling indebted to them because they accepted it, and you don't make people feel they owe you anything. You don't give something away because the other person needs it but because you have plenty and want to share. Just like the sun, you have in abundance, and you give away without asking for anything back.

Truthfulness

In Sufism, truthfulness is more profound than honesty. You become an embodiment of the truth. Even the most honest people can tell lies. People stick to the truth when it benefits them, even if it gets others in trouble. However, if their interests are compromised, they resort to lying. One can't be honest only when it suits them. Even the saying "honesty is the best policy" holds a negative meaning to it. It indicates that honesty is optional, which isn't the case. Being truthful is the correct way of living life, it's who you are. You become truthful when you understand that lying isn't an option and that the truth matters more than the consequences. You would rather risk everything for the truth than tell a lie.

Teachings of Sufism

Sufism teaches us to look deep within ourselves and find our truest selves and understand how to live life. It also instructs us to live in harmony with everything in existence. These teachings make Sufism a universal belief and not a just part of Islam. Sufism transcends religions, time, cultures, languages, and societies.

Love is one of Sufism's main teachings, and Sufis believe that "God is the Lover and the Beloved." All that a Sufi want is to give in to God. They want to love Him with all their beings and feel His love.

Muslim Sufis believe that Prophet Mohamed (peace be upon him) is the embodiment of perfection. They look up to him, hoping they can worship God as he did.

Sufism also includes other teachings, many of which can be embraced outside Islam.

- One must return to their childlike innocence to experience enlightenment

- Focus on nature and the Divine and let go of the material and physical attachments

- Pay attention to your dreams; they are trying to teach you something

- Love and serve others selflessly without expecting anything in return

- Keep your heart open, especially when you are praying

- There is only one God, and mankind are His children

- Love God by loving all His creations

- All religions must be respected as they are methods to reach the Divine

- Always choose peace and love, never violence

Practices of Sufism

Sufis practice their beliefs in mosques, shrines, or Dargahs (shrines built over Sufi saints in India). Orders usually meet in a majlis, an Arabic word for "sitting room." The majlis takes place in a khanqah, a Persian word, or zawiya, an Arabic word, and both refer to Muslim Sufi places of worship. You can practice Sufism alone or with a group of people. Mosques are very common in Muslim countries, and you can probably find a mosque in every town. Dargahs are only popular in India.

Dhikr

Dhikr is one of the main practices of Sufism. It is an Arabic word that means "remembering God." This practice was inspired by the Quran, which commands that all Muslims should always remember Allah. According to Islam, Dhikr makes you aware of God. You can practice Dhikr by praying, repeating verses of the Quran or hadiths, or simply repeating any of God's names. Some orders practice dhikr by singing, dancing, playing music, or meditating. Dhikr is practiced solo or in ceremonies.

Group dhikr is performed out loud. The shaykh usually says the lines, and his students repeat them after him. They can repeat the shahadah or the word "Allah" with their students in sync. Dhikr isn't optional but is an obligation in Islam. Muslim Sufis believe that any of the five pillars of Islam, like fasting or praying, are a form of dhikr since they focus on being aware of the Divine. Each tariqa practices dhikr differently, depending on the founder of the order.

In Judaism, a practice called Zakhor is quite similar to Dhikr where one remembers God.

Muraqaba

Muraqaba, Tamarkoz in Persian, is a form of meditation in Sufism. It is a very popular practice among Sufi practitioners. Just like its Arabic meaning, Muraqaba is to observe one's thoughts and be in control of one's desires. You focus your senses and your mind on a Quranic verse or the name of God until there is nothing and none in your thoughts but Allah. Muraqaba is inspired by Prophet Mohamed (peace be upon him). Before he was introduced to Islam and met Gabriel (an archangel sent by Allah), the Prophet practiced Muraqaba in the cave of Hira.

Hadhra

"Hadhra" is an Arabic word that means "presence." It is a dance that is usually practiced during dhikr, and it's more common in Arab countries. The purpose of hadhra and similar practices that involve singing is to plead for the presence of the angels, prophets, or the Divine.

Khalwa

Khalwa is an Arabic word that means "solitude." This practice involves retreating from society and being alone with your thoughts so you can focus on the Divine. The Murshid can advise his Murids to go on a Khalwa if he feels they will benefit from the solitude. Islamic traditions also inspired this practice. Muslims believe that Maryam (the Virgin Mary) and many other prophets retreated from the world and lived in solitude for some time. Prophet Mohamed (peace be upon him) practiced Muraqaba during his Khalwas in the cave of Hira. During a Khalwa, the prophet met Gabriel for the first time and received his first inspiration from Allah. The Prophet Moses also retreated from society and spent forty days in seclusion on Mount Sinai. The Virgin Mary spent a year in solitude in a Jewish temple, but the Prophet Zakariya was allowed to visit her.

Back in the day, Khalwa was a very popular practice, but it has become less common now since retreating from society and living in seclusion isn't practical as people now have jobs and other responsibilities they can't simply ignore.

Qawwali

Qawwali is derived from the Arabic word "qawl," which means a saying, and here it refers to Prophet

Mohamed's (peace be upon him) sayings. The practice involves singing devotional songs like praising God or the prophet and expressing one's love and devotion to Allah. Qawwali originated in India, and most of the lyrics are in Urdu, Hindi, or Persian language. It isn't practiced in the Arab world as it is more common in Turkey, Iran, Afghanistan, Pakistan, and India.

Sema

Sema is another Sufi practice that involves singing and dancing. It is practiced among the Uyghur (an ethnic group in China) and other cultures where practitioners perform specific dance moves to connect with the Divine. The dance originated from the Mevlevi order, whose followers practiced a type of whirling dancing. The dance moves represent the happiness and fulfillment one feels on their journey of connecting with the Divine and finding His love. They also symbolize the ascending of consciousness to a high level to reach God. Practitioners dance to music played on drums and reeds. The moves keep intensifying with the music until they reach a state of trance with their mind and body.

Sema is also very popular in Turkey. Practitioners wear white robes, sing, and dance in circular movements with rhythmic breathing. There is a different version of this practice that is quite popular in the Chishtiya order in India. In South Asia, practitioners dance to the music of the Qawwali.

This dance is one of the most powerful practices of Sufism. The practitioners go into a state of trance where they travel through a journey that transforms them completely.

Sufism's pillars and teachings show the world as black or white. You are only truthful when you completely refrain from lying; the concept of white lies doesn't exist in Sufism. It also showcases humility in a different light, where you must be completely honest with yourself and understand the ego to release it.

All of Sufism's practices and beliefs are meant to help you reach God and experience his love. The belief focuses on being good and loving the Divine by showing kindness and compassion to all His creation.

Chapter 3

Sufi Psychology

The foundations of Sufi psychology derive from the innate understanding held by Sufi mystics regarding the progression of an individual's spiritual path. They are mainly centered around the cultivation of the inner knowledge and spiritual development of an individual, with a focus on attaining spiritual enlightenment through methods distinct from traditional religious concepts. One core tenets of Sufi psychology is the purification of the self, which involves eliminating negative thoughts and emotions to reach a state of inner peace and tranquility. This chapter will explore the fundamental concepts and practices of Sufi psychology, its relationship with the human psyche, the concept of the ego, and the various aspects of this spiritual discipline. Additionally, it will examine how mastering these aspects can aid in the attainment of spiritual enlightenment and self-realization.

The main premise of Sufi psychology is the belief that the ultimate goal of our existence is to achieve a complete union with the divine. It is believed that the cultivation of sacred practices and inner knowledge can help develop one's spiritual abilities and reinforce their connection with the divine. According to Sufi beliefs, there are three facets to the human psyche: the ego, the heart, and the soul. In Sufi terminology, these facets are referred to as the Nafs, Qalb, and Ruh, respectively. The ego, or Nafs, is considered the baser aspect of one's personality, and it is deemed necessary to exert control over it. The nafs (ego) is responsible for worldly desires and attachments. The heart, or Qalb, serves as the nexus between the Nafs and the Ruh and is responsible for fostering spiritual understanding and knowledge. The Ruh or soul is perhaps the most important aspect of one's personality. It is believed that mastering this aspect of one's existence can help achieve spiritual enlightenment.

Spiritual growth and enlightenment are strongly emphasized in Sufism, and a variety of methods are employed to progress spiritually, including prayers, meditation, and studies of sacred texts. A special emphasis is also placed on one's spiritual master or mentor. One of the main aspects of Sufi psychology incorporates the concept that the ego has to be annihilated to move further in one's spiritual journey. This is done through a number of methods, which will be discussed later in the chapter.

The Facets of Sufi Psychology

The transcendental aspects of Sufi psychology encompass the heart, the self, and the soul. These terms should not be understood in their conventional sense but rather as metaphysical constructs. These concepts have their roots in Quranic scripture and require a deep understanding for one to progress on their spiritual journey.

1. Nafs

In Sufi psychology, the concept of Nafs is multifaceted and pertains to the inner self or ego. It is regarded as a central construct in comprehending the human psyche and the quest for spiritual enlightenment. In Sufism, the Nafs is perceived as a catalyst for worldly desires and a builder of the ego. It can also be understood as an individual's self-perception or self-identity.

It is believed that the Nafs is in a constant state of struggle between good and evil. It can be the origin of many negative thoughts and traits, such as greed, selfishness, pride, and anger. These negative aspects can lead to destructive behaviors and thoughts and impede spiritual fulfillment. Therefore, it is crucial to cleanse and exert control over the Nafs.

This is achieved through spiritual practices such as meditation, self-realization activities, prayer, and self-reflection. These practices enable individuals to gain a deeper understanding of themselves and their negative traits and to work towards transcending these negative aspects to reach a higher state of mind characterized by peace, contentment, and tranquility.

Tazkiyah is also an important aspect of Sufi psychology as it focuses on eliminating negative thoughts and cultivating positive emotions such as compassion, humility, and self-awareness. This purification method is not just limited to the individual's emotional well-being but also their physical and spiritual health. A common way this is achieved is through "dhikr," or remembrance of the divine.

2. Qalb

In Sufi psychology, the concept of Qalb, or heart, is considered to be the central aspect of the self and the soul. It is believed to be the intermediary between the individual's inner self and their spiritual connection with the divine. In this context, the heart does not refer to the physical organ but rather is viewed as the center of the soul that connects the individual with the divine.

The Qalb is also believed to be the mirror of one's soul, reflecting one's true nature and connection with the divine. It is seen as the source of spiritual growth and understanding and the place where the individual can gain a direct understanding of God. Through the purification of the heart, known as "tazkiyah al-qalb," it is believed that the individual can remove obstacles that impede their ability to experience the presence of God in the heart, mind, and soul.

Sufis engage in spiritual practices to purify their hearts. These techniques assist a person in developing a better understanding of their negative tendencies and how to transcend them to achieve a higher mental state characterized by peace, contentment, and tranquility.

3. Ruh

In Sufi psychology, the concept of Ruh, or the soul, is considered to be the connecting force between the individual and the divine. The soul is viewed as the embodiment of spiritual energy and the key to attaining spiritual awakening. Through understanding and transcending this aspect of the personality, an individual can ultimately move toward spiritual fulfillment. The Ruh is often referred to as the "breath of light" that connects the divine with the living, animating humans and linking them to God.

Sufi spiritual practices are believed to aid in the purification of the Ruh and the understanding of one's place in the world. Unlike other aspects of the self, the soul is directly connected with the divine, even if the individual is unaware of this connection. The ultimate goal is to transcend the levels of the soul and become aware of one's divine connection.

In Sufism, the Ruh is believed to have seven facets that make up the holistic nature of a person. These include the mineral, vegetable, animal, personal, human, secret, and secret of secrets souls. Each of these levels reflects the stages of its evolution and has strengths, weaknesses, and gifts associated with them. To balance the soul, an individual must develop the strengths associated with each level while minimizing the weaknesses. It is also important to achieve a balance between the lower and upper levels and focus on all of them equally.

In the context of Sufi psychology, the concept of the human psyche is understood to be composed of three interconnected aspects that work in harmony to assist individuals in attaining spiritual enlightenment. These aspects reflect the diverse experiences of humanity and are considered essential for spiritual understanding and development. Through the practice of spiritual disciplines, an individual can purify and exert control over the Nafs, cleanse their heart or Qalb, and deepen their connection with the divine through the Ruh.

Jihad in Sufism

Contrary to the popularly held perception of Jihad as a concept, within the context of Sufism, it pertains to an individual's spiritual or internal struggle against their own Nafs or egoistic desires. This inner battle against one's impulses is considered the most arduous form of Jihad in Islam. In comparison, the Lesser Jihad, which encompasses physical warfare and struggles against external adversaries, is deemed relatively effortless. This is because resisting one's self is inherently more challenging than exerting control over the actions of others. Nevertheless, this is the path to attaining spiritual enlightenment and self-awareness.

In Sufism, Jihad is viewed as an ongoing process of self-improvement that requires exceptional self-control, discipline, consistency, and a steadfast commitment to spiritual practices such as meditation, introspection, and prayer. Only by engaging in this internal struggle can one attain true purification of their soul, ultimately leading to a deeper understanding of the world and the divine. Notably, in Sufism, Jihad is not solely associated with the Nafs but also with the purification of the Qalb and the Ruh. Once an individual has achieved mastery over their Nafs, their path toward spiritual enlightenment becomes clear, and they must undertake the purification of the Qalb and the Ruh to attain a connection with God. This is why Jihad ul-Nafs is considered one of the most vital aspects of Sufism.

The Levels of Nafs

As previously mentioned, the attainment of true enlightenment necessitates the transcendence of a series of stages of Nafs. These stages, referred to as the seven levels of Nafs, are deemed crucial for the cultivation of one's spiritual identity and comprehension.

1. Nafs-e-Ammara

In the pursuit of spiritual enlightenment, it is essential to transcend the initial stage of Nafs, known as Nafs-e-Ammara. This stage is referred to as the "commanding soul," which encompasses weaker desires or negative impulses that an individual may be inclined towards, such as greed, selfishness, or a lack of self-control. This stage of Nafs is in constant opposition to divine teachings and is dominated by the ego.

2. Nafs-e-Lawwama

The second stage of Nafs referred to as Nafs-e-Lawwama or the "accusing soul," is associated with one's conscience, self-awareness, guilt, and remorse. At this stage, the individual begins to acknowledge the need for change and spiritual growth, marking the onset of the internal struggle against the self.

3. Nafs-e-Mulhama

As the purification stage of the Nafs commences, the individual reaches the third stage, known as Nafs-e-Mulhama or the "censured soul." This stage is characterized by feelings of uncertainty and doubt about one's journey, leading the individual to seek guidance from spiritual mentors and teachers.

4. Nafs-e-Mardiyya

The fourth stage, referred to as Nafs-e-Mardiyya or the "pleased soul," marks the beginning of the spiritual journey. At this stage, the individual becomes gratuitous, humble, and content, but not to the point of stagnation in their spiritual development. In this stage, a deeper understanding of the divine and a stronger connection with God begins to take shape.

5. Nafs-e-Sakiyya

As spiritual maturity is attained, the individual reaches the fifth stage, known as Nafs-e-Sakiyya or the "satisfied soul." This stage is associated with feelings of peace, tranquility, and harmony, and the individual begins to comprehend their place in the world.

6. Nafs-e-Mutmainna

The sixth stage, known as Nafs-e-Mutmainna or the "content soul," is characterized by near spiritual enlightenment and feelings of self-awareness, inner peace, and a profound connection with the divine.

7. Nafs-e-Radiyya

The seventh and final stage of Nafs referred to as Nafs-e-Radiyya or the "pleased stage of God," represents the attainment of spiritual perfection. At this stage, the individual realizes their full spiritual potential and reaches the ultimate goal of spiritual development, characterized by complete ease and unity with the divine, though it is acknowledged that this stage may be difficult to reach.

It's important to note that these stages aren't necessarily linear in nature and can be experienced at different points in life. Most people go through these stages at different times and under different circumstances in their lives. However, the ultimate goal is always to reach the seventh stage, which is filled with spiritual satisfaction, inner peace, and spiritual fulfillment.

In conclusion, Sufi psychology offers a comprehensive approach to spiritual cultivation, with a central focus on the purification of the self, the transcendence of the ego, and the attainment of spiritual enlightenment through the cultivation of inner knowledge and sacred practices. The guidance of a spiritual mentor, or "shaykh" or "pir," is deemed a fundamental element in this discipline, as they possess the expertise and wisdom to assist individuals in navigating the complexities of their spiritual journey. Furthermore, the foundations of Sufi psychology emphasize the cultivation of spiritual development and inner knowledge through various religious and Sufi practices, with the ultimate goal being the realization of a complete union with the divine. The chapter delved into the intricacies of this spiritual discipline, highlighting the methods and techniques that can aid individuals in achieving this ultimate goal.

Chapter 4

The Wing of Love

Sufism, as a spiritual practice, is predicated on the principle of love. Not only is it a recurring theme within this context, but it also serves as the fundamental foundation upon which the tenets of Sufism are built. Whether one considers their relationship with the Divine or their connection to the world, the concept of love is central to understanding the spiritual journey of the Sufi. It is viewed as the underlying premise of all spiritual practices, regardless of religious affiliation, and is deemed essential for attaining spiritual enlightenment. This chapter will delve into the intricacies of this powerful spiritual force and examine the ways in which it can be cultivated during one's spiritual journey.

Love in Sufism

Love, as a universal human experience, serves as the connective tissue that binds all individuals together and defines humanity. Therefore, Sufis seek to deepen their understanding of the Divine and the world through the cultivation of love, which in turn assists in transcending the ego and purifying the heart, as previously discussed. Furthermore, love is perceived as a transformative force capable of altering one's perception of the world and providing a renewed perspective. It is believed that love has the power to heal, change, and bring about spiritual awakening.

It is well-established that the ultimate aspiration of a spiritual journey is to attain a state of union with the divine, referred to as "Fana" in Arabic. As a central tenet, love plays a vital role in the pursuit of enlightenment. The transcendence of the self can only be accomplished through the integration of love into one's thought processes.

The Duality of Love: Two Wings of the Same Bird

In Sufism, love is recognized as a duality comprising two distinct wings. The first wing represents the veneration an individual holds towards the divine, referred to as "Ishq," which is considered the pinnacle of love. The second wing, "Mahabba," pertains to the love for God's creations. Both forms of love are deemed indispensable for attaining spiritual transcendence, as one cannot exist without the other. One who loves the divine must also love its creations, and conversely, one who loves the creations cannot help but love the divine. Thus, these two wings of love are the dual aspects, the spiritual and the worldly, that must be harmoniously cultivated to attain true spiritual enlightenment.

Love as Transcendent, Immanent, and Hidden Treasure

Sufism posits a plethora of nuanced concepts of love, each imbued with its unique and captivating intricacies. Love is perceived as transcendent, immanent, and a concealed treasure. These simple terms, however, encompass profound and complex interpretations. Love is transcendent in that it surpasses the physical realm, serving as the means by which one attains spiritual enlightenment. It is also considered immanent, as it is inherent in the very essence of all things, providing a glimpse of the divine in every aspect of existence, be it in the majestic mountains or the tranquil ocean. Love is also characterized as a concealed treasure, as it must be sought after and discovered through a process of purification, self-discovery, and inner struggle (nafs-e-jihad), which is difficult but ultimately leads to self-reflection and spiritual fulfillment. Thus, love serves as the key to unlocking the hidden secrets of the spiritual journey, and it is only through love that one can fully embark and complete the spiritual quest.

The Concepts of Ishq and Mahabba in Sufism

The cultivation and balance of Ishq and Mahabba are integral to attaining spiritual enlightenment. Ishq, the love of God, is deemed the paramount form of love in Sufism, characterized by an intense longing for the divine and a profound devotion to the Creator. This spiritual form of love enables an individual to detach from the material world and focus on a higher purpose. Concurrently, Mahabba, the love for all of God's creations, must be cultivated alongside Ishq. Without this love, one cannot fully appreciate the creations of the divine. Mahabba instills qualities such as compassion, generosity, and kindness towards all of God's creations and helps an individual to transcend their ego and gain a deeper understanding of the spiritual path. Both Ishq and Mahabba are vital for spiritual development as they facilitate the purification of the heart and soul and enable one to transcend the ego.

Inayat Khan and his Teachings on Love

Throughout history, numerous distinguished Sufi poets have conveyed the message of love through their artistic expressions. One such notable figure is Inayat Khan, a prominent Sufi mystic of the late 19th century. He is widely recognized as one of the most influential figures in the history of Sufism, and his teachings on love and spirituality are considered to be unique and profound. Inayat Khan believed that love forms the foundation of all spiritual practices and forms of worship and that by cultivating the appropriate forms of love, one can attain spiritual fulfillment through a connection with the divine. He was a key figure in shaping the principles of Sufism and emphasizing the importance of loving both God and His creations. His teachings on love continue to be widely studied and upheld to this day.

Love Poetry in Sufism: Expressions of the Divine

Artistic expression, including music, dance, calligraphy, art, and poetry, play a significant role in Sufism. Among these, the love poetry of renowned Sufi mystics has been particularly renowned for its emotive and evocative nature. Despite being primarily intended as a means of expressing devotion and love for the divine, these works of poetry have also profoundly impacted the spiritual perspectives of many readers. The themes of Sufi love poetry typically encompass spiritual and mystical concepts, often chronicling the authors' spiritual journeys and their longing for union with the divine.

These poets employ vivid imagery and elegant metaphors to convey their feelings of yearning and longing for the love of God. Their works also often depict the struggles, insights, and triumphs encountered on the spiritual path. The poetry of Rumi, Hafiz, Yunus Emre, and Inayat Khan is considered to be among the most profound and transformative expressions of love, devotion, and spirituality in literature. Furthermore, Sufi poetry is also frequently used as a form of spiritual practice, with individuals reciting, memorizing, and meditating upon various Sufi poems to facilitate their connection with God.

- **"The Conference of the Birds" by Farid ud-Din Attar**

This poem explores the allegorical journey of a congregation of birds as they seek their divine ruler. Along the way, the birds face a variety of obstacles, which serve as metaphorical representations of the challenges faced during one's spiritual quest. Ultimately, the birds discover that their king has been among them all along, symbolizing the realization that the divine resides within each individual.

- **"Divan-i-Hafiz" by Hafiz**

A beautiful collection of poems widely regarded as a pinnacle of Persian literature. The poems guide the reader through a series of spiritual journeys, utilizing vivid imagery and metaphorical language to convey the poet's belief that love is the path to the divine.

- **"Masnavi" by Rumi**

One of the most renowned poems by one of the most notable poets, Masnavi by Rumi, is a splendid collection of Sufi poems that are filled with parables and stories that symbolize the spiritual teachings and wisdom of Sufism. Most of these poems conveyed Rumi's message about love and God's path.

- **"The Love Poems" by Yunus Emre**

The renowned 13th-century Turkish poet authored this collection of poems, and delves into the poet's mystical experiences and unyielding devotion to the divine. The collection reflects the poet's personal musings on the theme of love in the context of his relationship with the divine and its earthly manifestation. The poems, known for their candid and emotive language, are widely celebrated for their simplicity, emotional intensity, and honesty and are considered to be foundational in the development of Turkish Sufism.

- **"The Inner Life" by Inayat Khan**

Inayat Khan had many collections of love poems, but "The Inner Life" collection is among the best Sufi poems. These love poems expound on the significance of ishq and mohabbat as the foundation of all spiritual practices. And are known for their nuanced exploration of spiritual concepts.

These poetic works, authored by Sufi poets, are not merely literary creations but rather a medium through which the poets' profound devotion to the divine is articulated and conveyed. These works serve as a means of spiritual connection, offering the reader an opportunity to contemplate the transcendent nature of love and devotion and gain insight into the mystical experiences of the poets. They are an integral part of the Sufi literary tradition and a testament to the enduring connection between the human and the divine.

Love as a Path to Spiritual Awakening: Staying on the Sufi Way

In Sufi tradition, the concept of balancing the wing of love encompasses not only the expression of one's love for the divine and the cultivation of a connection with the transcendent but also the steadfast adherence to the spiritual path towards ultimate fulfillment. Love is understood as a powerful means of purging negative thoughts and emotions and fostering positive ones. Guided by a spiritual mentor, you will be able to remain steadfastly focused on your journey and avoid the pitfalls of distraction, negative emotions, and obstacles. Love serves as an anchor, providing the motivation and commitment necessary to persevere on the path toward spiritual enlightenment.

In conclusion, the concepts of love and Sufism are inextricably intertwined. Love is a fundamental aspect of the Sufi way of life, and without it, spiritual enlightenment is unattainable. This essential principle has been emphasized by a plethora of renowned Sufi poets and scholars, such as Rumi, Inayat Khan, Hafiz, and many others. By nurturing love in one's existence, one can transcend the limitations of the ego and cultivate a deeper connection with the divine and, ultimately, the world.

Chapter 5

The Sufi Path

The purpose of Sufism is to make one better by connecting with the Divine. It brings gratitude, mercy, generosity, affection, and forgiveness into your life. By understanding the teachings and pillars of Sufism, you can understand these beautiful messages that can transform mankind. It aims to purify human beings of their sins and flaws and provide them with the qualities and attributes of Prophet Mohamed (Peace be upon him) and the other Prophets, which will enable them to experience the pleasure of feeling and seeing the Divine in everything they do.

When you apply the teachings of Sufism, you surrender your ego to God and let go of the material so your heart is pure and you can truly worship Allah. God gave human beings more advantages than any of His other creations. They are created on the fitra, which is their best nature. Instead of holding on to this beautiful nature, mankind keeps steering away from it and from Allah's teachings. They corrupt their spirit and become a bad version of themselves. Sufism brings you back to this nature and reminds you of your faith.

Sufis follow the teachings of Prophet Mohamed (Peace be upon him) as Sufism urges them to follow his lead. Following in the footsteps of the prophets protects you from desires and temptations mankind is subjected to in their everyday lives. Sufism also helps people with pure souls to stay on the right path. When you let go of the material, cleanse yourself of your sins, and follow the right path, you will establish a spiritual awakening,

It isn't an exaggeration to say that Sufism can save your soul. Practicing this belief will purge you and push you to be good and perform righteous deeds, which God has instructed all His believers to do. Whether you are a Muslim or not, practicing Sufism inspires you to live a moral life and make the right choices because it is the only path to the Divine. It serves as a reminder to be good and do better. You focus on satisfying your soul instead of your physical gratifications.

The Four Spiritual Paths of Sufism

One can't achieve spiritual awakening without walking on the right paths. There are four paths or doors in Sufism. You begin the journey through sharia, then move to tariqa, and then acquire haqiqa, which will lead you to ma'rifah.

Sharia

Shaira is the first of the four paths, and it is referred to as the correct path. It is a group of divine laws that every Muslim should follow to live an honest life and become close to Allah. All the sharia laws come from the teachings of the Quran and Hadiths. The interpretation of sharia is called "fiqh," and it was established after the death of Prophet Mohamed (Peace be upon him).

Although sharia is commonly described as "Islamic laws," some scholars interpret it differently. They believe that it is the word of God and refers to strict divine values and the will of God that mankind doesn't know or understand. On the other hand, Islamic laws are derived from sharia. You can't study sharia without knowledge of the Quran and Sunnah (practices of Prophet Mohamed, Peace be upon him).

Sufis and Muslims consider sharia as a way of living life. It constitutes how one should properly worship God. Worshipping God includes practicing the five pillars of Islam, which Sufis believe doesn't only get them closer to God but also leads them to achieve spiritual awakening. Praying five times a day, fasting in the month of Ramadan, giving Zakat, performing Hajj, and other Islamic practices involve remembering God or the practice of dhikr. Dhikr is the key to reaching a higher level of consciousness and awakening your spirit.

Sufis believe that true happiness lies in experiencing the Divine's love. According to the Islamic laws of sharia, Prophet Mohamed (Peace be upon him) teaches Muslims that you can only know your place in God's eyes by looking inward and seeing where you hold God in your heart. To truly love God is to constantly remember Him.

Naturally, you will encounter temptations in life, but the person who keeps God on their mind will think twice before sinning or giving in to their desires. Dhikr will always bring your awareness to the Divine and remind you that steering from the path of God will deprive you of His love.

According to sharia and Islamic teachings, one should be kind to others. Whether it's your family, friends, co-workers, or neighbors, treating everyone with love and compassion is how you become closer to God and achieve Sufism's goal.

Follow the laws of sharia to open your heart to the Divine.

- Believe in God and follow His teaching
- Worship God by following the five Pillars of Islam
- Do what is right and steer clear of what is wrong
- Treat others with compassion
- Follow the Sunnah

Once you apply sharia teaching in your life, you will be ready to walk through the second path.

Tariqah

Tariqa is the second path of Sufism, and one can only walk through it after fully understanding sharia and applying its teachings. Tariqa refers to the different schools of Sufism or orders. The Tariqa consists of different orders; each one has its own rules and tasks. Similar to the Madhhabs (schools of thought) of Islam, orders must have Imams (leaders in Islam).

There are various Tariqas all over the world. Each person can join the order they feel drawn to or one that fulfills their needs. One joins a Tariqa to go on a spiritual journey and achieve Sufism's purpose by reaching the Divine. When looking for a Tariqa, don't expect to find a rating system or a comparison between the orders. In other words, there isn't a good or bad Tariqa. Each one is different and has its own characteristics. No Tariqa tries to stand out or prove that it is better since there is no competition among the orders of Sufism.

You can't go on your Tariqa path without first finishing the sharia one. Scholars often compare the relationship between these paths with that of a ship and sea. Sharia is the ship that one must step on for the journey into the sea, which is Tariqa. Sharia is the set of laws in Islam, while tariqa is the spiritual path that takes one on a journey to expand their knowledge of God. It is every Sufi's obligation to seek knowledge.

All reputable and legitimate orders don't accept mureeds who don't understand the sharia. Once they do and become a member of an order, their murshid will give them dhikr to practice every day.

Tariqa and sharia are different. Some people confuse the two, which can lead them to join an order without bothering to learn about the sharia. Sharia acts as the foundation on which Tariqa builds its practices. For instance, the Dhikr practice is based on the sharia teachings of remembering God. Without learning sharia, the Sufis wouldn't have been able to come up with many of their practices. In other words, tariqa is the path that you take to experience the spiritual side of sharia.

Sema is one of the most common practices in tariqa as it originated from its most popular order, the Mevlevi order. Through the intense dance moves, one can experience a trance and reach the Divine.

Here are some of the tariqa's teachings that will connect you with the divine.

- Repenting your mistakes and cleansing your soul to prepare for the Divine's love
- Resisting temptation

- Helping others
- Learning from others
- Being charitable

It is essential to note that Sufism and Islam encourage thinking and using one's brain. So, if you encounter an order, a murshid, or a shaykh that expects blind obedience from you or forces you to perform a practice you aren't comfortable with, walk away, as this order may be trying to exploit you.

Haqiqa

Haqiqa or haqiqat is an Arabic word that means truth, and it's the third path one must walk through after sharia and tariqa. The purpose of the tariqa is to unveil the haqiqa or ultimate truth for you. However, as a concept, haqiqa isn't easy to define. Some scholars define it as everything true, real, authentic, and genuine in a metaphysical sense. This definition explains the concept of haqiqa but still doesn't clarify its role in Sufism.

Haqiqa is the knowledge you gain after you connect with the Divine. You gain this knowledge after taking the tariqa path. The shaykhs, in orders, usually acquire haqiqa through advancing in the chains of tariqa and can then pass this knowledge on to their students.

Through haqiqa, one can gain knowledge of the unknown. For instance, a shaykh can know if one of his students is sick or getting married before they tell him. Haqiqa opens your eyes to learn the Divine's secrets. It gives you insight into the meta-physical world, which only occurs after you establish a close relationship with God. However, haqiqa must be based on sharia, or it will be meaningless.

Some argue that haqiqa isn't a path or stage but a higher level of consciousness which you need before reaching the final path. In Sufism, haqiqa is more of a phase that is essential to the ones seeking answers to life's biggest questions. You can establish haqiqa by practicing muraqaba, as meditation can transcend your consciousness. Practicing musha-hida can bring you close to God so you can reach the ultimate truth. Mushahida, which roughly translates to "witness," is observing the Divine. Su-fis spend their whole lives searching for God, who can't be acquired without mushahida and being present with the Divine. When you experience God's love, you can observe Him and reach haqiqa. However, unveiling or witnessing the Divine face is an extreme punishment in Sufism.

Haqiqa's teachings include:

- Practicing compassion and mercy
- Not focusing on other people's flaws
- Accepting that there is only one God
- Sharing your knowledge with others

Ma'rifah

Ma'rifah is an Arabic word that means knowledge and refers to the knowledge of God. It is the last path that one goes through after elevating your consciousness through haqiqa. Ma'rifah is the treasure you find in the sea of tariqa after getting on the ship of sharia. It is the gift you get after walking through the three paths of Sufism. You obtain this mystical knowledge through tariqa as a reward for surrendering to the sharia and obeying the Divine.

One can gain ma'rifah through introspection and reflection. Ma'rifah is different from scientific knowledge because it requires you to use your intuition, while science requires you to look outward to analyze and investigate. If one doesn't have ma'rifah, they won't be considered ignorant, but they will be living in denial.

Regular knowledge is different from ma'rifah. Ma'rifah isn't the understanding of something; it is recognizing and familiarizing yourself with the concept of the Divine. However, it isn't enough to just know God; you should know all the ways that can lead to Him. Be aware that you will encounter obstacles on your way to the Divine. Only those who can overcome any hardships can reach ma'rifah.

Sufis regard the person who has ma'rifah as a perfect human being. Reaching perfection is one of the goals of Sufism that can be attained on this path. Through ma'rifah, you can lead a moral life just like the Prophets and feel the Divine's light in everything you do.

One can acquire ma'rifah by practicing khalwa or muraqaba, as both allow you to remain focused and look within yourself to find the Divine. You must also keep your heart cleansed and your intentions pure.

You can reach ma'rifah by

- Truly knowing yourself
- Gaining knowledge and sharing it with others
- Being patient
- Having morals

Sufism is a journey, and you can't reach your destination without walking through its four paths. Each path brings you closer to attaining spiritual awakening. Before choosing a Tariqa that fits your personality and needs, you should first learn everything about sharia. Tariqa will take you on a spiritual path to haqiqa, where you will reach a higher level of consciousness that will prepare you for the final path, Ma'rifah, and gain knowledge of the Divine. Through this knowledge, one can accomplish Sufi's main purpose and become closer to the Divine, which is how you can achieve spiritual awakening.

Conclusion

Muslims and non-Muslims have embraced Sufism and its teaching. Sufism is a universal belief that many people find relevant to their lives. With everything happening in the world right now, we all need to spread the message of love, which is what Sufism provides.

We began this book by explaining Sufism and its relationship with Islam. Although scholars can't agree on the true origin of Sufism, it still has a very rich and fascinating history that we provided in this book. We also introduced some of Sufism's terminology to familiarize you with the concept better. People practice Sufism to get closer to God. This book introduced the spiritual beliefs associated with it and how people use them to reach the Divine.

Many people misunderstand Sufism and think that it is the same as Islam. While Sufis believe it is connected with Islam, it is different from Sunni and Shia. We ended the chapter by explaining how Sufism stands out from Islam sects.

There are a reason millions of people around the world practice Sufism. The belief's teachings and practices can take you on a journey that won't only connect you with God but will change your perception and transform you. We introduced you to all Sufism practices and how people use them to worship God.

Sufism isn't just a spiritual faith. Its association with psychology has fascinated people all over the world. We explained the different aspects of psychology in Sufism and introduced the concept of Jihad. We also introduced the concept of self-realization and the different stages one has to go through to attain it.

Sufism is love, and Sufis interpret this feeling in a more profound way. We explained the different concepts and terms associated with love and how Sufis believe that only through love can one reach spiritual awakening.

The purpose of Sufism is to connect us with the Divine. We ended the book by explaining the paths of Sufism and how they can help you achieve your goal and reach God.

Analyst, M. A. S. (n.d.). What is Sufism? Institute for Global Change. https://institute.global/policy/what-sufism

Bissada, A.-M. (2018, January 27). What is Sufism, and why does it bother some Muslims? RFI. https://www.rfi.fr/en/middle-east/20180127-what-sufism-and-why-does-it-bother-some-muslims

Bjerregaard, C. H. A. (2015a). Sufism: Omar Khayyam and E. fitzgerald. Andesite Press.

Bjerregaard, C. H. A. (2015b). Sufism: Omar Khayyam and E. fitzgerald. Andesite Press.

Corbin, T. (2022, May 4). Spirituality in Islam - How is it Different from Other Faiths? About Islam. https://aboutislam.net/spirituality/spirituality-islam-how-is-it-different-from-other-faiths/

History of Sufism. (2019, July 15). The Spiritual Life. https://slife.org/history-of-sufism/

Jasūr Magazine. (2021, February 27). The Dichotomous (MIS)understanding of Sufism — Jasūr Magazine. Jasūr Magazine. https://jasurmagazine.org/politics-policy/sufi-islam-heresy-or-a-counter-narrative-to-extremism

Knott, K. (2016, June 9). What are the Five Pillars of Islam? Crestresearch.ac.uk. https://crestresearch.ac.uk/comment/islam-five-pillars/

Major beliefs and practices of Sufism. (2022, January 22). GeeksforGeeks. https://www.geeksforgeeks.org/major-beliefs-and-practices-of-sufism/

Malik, S. (2011, June 25). What is Sufism? The Threshold Society - Mevlevi Sufi Order; The Threshold Society. https://sufism.org/sufism

Mazid, M. A. (2021, December 16). Mawlana Jalal-ad-din Muhammad Rumi and Sufism. The Business Standard. https://www.tbsnews.net/thoughts/mawlana-jalal-ad-din-muhammad-rumi-and-sufism-344788

Pruitt, S. (2019, July 31). Islam's Sunni-Shia divide, explained. HISTORY. https://www.history.com/news/sunni-shia-divide-islam-muslim

RumiClub. (n.d.). Umass.edu. https://www.umass.edu/gso/rumi/rumi3.htm

Schimmel, A. (2022). Sufism. In Encyclopedia Britannica.

Shaykh. (n.d.). Patheos.com. https://www.patheos.com/library/glossary/shaykh

Specia, M. (2017, November 24). Who are Sufi Muslims and why do some extremists hate them? The New York Times. https://www.nytimes.com/2017/11/24/world/middleeast/sufi-muslim-explainer.html

Super User. (n.d.). The origins of Sufism. Sufiway.org. https://www.sufiway.org/about-us/the-origins-of-sufism

The Editors of Encyclopedia Britannica. (2022). Sunni. In Encyclopedia Britannica.

Winter, C. (2017, November 25). Sufi Islam: What you need to know. Deutsche Welle. https://www.dw.com/en/sufi-islam-what-you-need-to-know/a-41532401

Yadav, C. (2021, July 7). Difference between Sunni and Sufi. Ask Any Difference. https://askanydifference.com/difference-between-sunni-and-sufi/

A mysticism that birthed some of the world's most profound poets. (n.d.). Gaia. https://www.gaia.com/article/the-beautiful-teachings-of-sufism-and-the-sufi-saints

A mysticism that birthed some of the world's most profound poets. (n.d.). Gaia. https://www.gaia.com/article/the-beautiful-teachings-of-sufism-and-the-sufi-saints

Analyst, M. A. S. (n.d.). What is Sufism? Institute for Global Change. https://institute.global/policy/what-sufism

Bjerregaard, C. H. A. (2015). Sufism: Omar Khayyam and E. fitzgerald. Andesite Press.

Jasūr Magazine. (2021, February 27). The Dichotomous (MIS)understanding of Sufism — Jasūr Magazine. Jasūr Magazine. https://jasurmagazine.

org/politics-policy/sufi-islam-heresy-or-a-counter-narrative-to-extremism

Katju, M. (2014, July 7). Dargahs and Sufis. Times of India. https://timesofindia.indiatimes.com/blogs/satyam-bruyat/dargahs-and-sufis/

Osho, D. (2006, August 5). The three pillars of Sufism: Humility, charity, truth. Times Of India. https://timesofindia.indiatimes.com/edit-page/the-three-pillars-of-sufism-humility-charity-truth/articleshow/1855384.cms

(N.d.-a). Brainly.In. https://brainly.in/question/3971482

(N.d.-b). Washingtonpost.com. https://www.washingtonpost.com/world/2022/04/30/afghanistan-sufi-mosque-blast/

Hamzah, H. (n.d.). PSYCHOLOGY and ISLAM. Blogspot.com. http://spychology-of-islam.blogspot.com/2012/01/heart-self-and-soul-concepts-in.html

Levels of the self. (2002, June 9). The Threshold Society - Mevlevi Sufi Order. https://sufism.org/sufism/writings-on-sufism/levels-of-the-self-2

Porzelt, B. (n.d.). Your seven souls: A Sufi view. Theosophical Society in America. https://www.theosophical.org/publications/quest-magazine/1590-your-seven-souls-a-sufi-view

Helminski, K. (2012, November 30). Be in Love. The Threshold Society - Mevlevi Sufi Order. https://sufism.org/library/articles/be-in-love

Kelly, M. (n.d.). Love in Sufi poetry. Fountainmagazine.com. https://fountainmagazine.com/2012/issue-87-may-june-2012/love-in-sufi-poetry-may-june-2012

Sufi Poetry. (n.d.). Wahiduddin.net. https://wahiduddin.net/sufi/sufi_poetry.htm

The teachings of Inayat khan. (2022, February 5). Toward The One; Inayati Order of Austin. https://towardtheone.com/the-teachings-of-inayat-khan/

(N.d.). Questionsonislam.com. https://questionsonislam.com/article/what-love-terms-sufism

Dewji, N. (2015, October 8). Sufism aims the individual to a spiritual awakening through prayer and devotion. Ismailimail. https://ismailimail.blog/2015/10/08/sufism-aims-the-individual-to-a-spiritual-awakening-through-prayer-and-devotion/

Four Doors. (n.d.). Wikiwand. https://www.wikiwand.com/en/Four_Doors

Grayce, K. (2015). A spiritual awakening: Finding your connection. WestBow Press.

Gülen, F. (2007, July 14). Ma'rifa (knowledge of god). Fgulen.com. http://fgulen.com/en/fethullah-gulens-works/key-concepts-in-the-practice-of-sufism-2/marifa-knowledge-of-god

Gülen, F. (2015, January 5). Haqq (the truth), haqiqa (the genuine) and what lies beyond. Fgulen.com. http://fgulen.com/en/fethullah-gulens-works/key-concepts-in-the-practice-of-sufism-4/haqq-the-truth-haqiqa-the-genuine-and-what-lies-beyond

Haqiqat. (2019, July 16). The Spiritual Life. https://slife.org/haqiqat/

Ma'rifa (knowledge of God). (2019, September 3). The Spiritual Life. https://slife.org/marifa-knowledge-of-god/

Ma'rifa (Spiritual Knowledge of God). (2019, August 21). The Spiritual Life. https://slife.org/marifa-spiritual-knowledge-of-god/

Robinson, K. (2005, April 25). Understanding sharia: The intersection of Islam and the law. Council on Foreign Relations. https://www.cfr.org/backgrounder/understanding-sharia-intersection-islam-and-law

Spiritual Awakening and the future of our world. (2013, January 22). IslamiCity; Human Assistance & Develop Intl. https://www.islamicity.org/5113/spiritual-awakening-and-the-future-of-our-world/

Tamim, H. (2021, August 3). Should you follow a tariqa? Utrujj. https://www.utrujj.org/should-you-follow-a-tariqa/

The Editors of Encyclopedia Britannica. (2020). tariqa. In Encyclopedia Britannica.

Topbaş, O. N. (2011, May 2). The aim of Sufism. Osman Nuri Topbas | Official Page in English; Osman Nuri Topbas. https://en.osmannuritopbas.com/the-aim-of-sufism.html

Understanding Sufi tariqas. (n.d.). Aqrtsufi.org. https://www.aqrtsufi.org/sufism/tariqas.html

What is tariqa? (2019, July 16). The Spiritual Life. https://slife.org/tariqa/

What is Tariqa and Shari`ah? What is the difference between them? (n.d.). Islam.Ru. https://www.islam.ru/en/content/story/what-tariqa-and-shari-ah-what-difference-between-them

Wormald, B. (2013, April 30). Chapter 1: Beliefs about sharia. Pew Research Center's Religion & Public Life Project. https://www.pewresearch.org/religion/2013/04/30/the-worlds-muslims-religion-politics-society-beliefs-about-sharia

* 9 7 9 8 2 1 5 7 2 6 4 2 6 *